SLIP, SKID, AND RUN

THE UNTOLD CAUSE OF THE INDIANAPOLIS RAMADA INN CRASH

SLIP, SKID, AND RUN

THE UNTOLD CAUSE OF THE INDIANAPOLIS RAMADA INN CRASH

MARK F. MURRAY

WITH MEGIN E. MURRAY
EDITING BY JIM SCOTTI

proving press

Disclaimer: The views expressed herein and those of the author and do not reflect the official positions of the Department of Defense or any other agency of the United States Government.

Book Design & Production:
Columbus Publishing Lab
www.ColumbusPublishingLab.com

Copyright © 2025 by
Mark F. Murray

All rights reserved.
This book, or parts thereof, may not be reproduced in any form without permission.

Paperback ISBN: 978-1-63337-985-5
E-Book ISBN: 978-1-63337-986-2

Printed in the United States of America
1 3 5 7 9 10 8 6 4 2

CONTENTS

PREFACE i

CHAPTER 1: THE UN-SILENT KNIGHT 1

CHAPTER 2: AVIATION ACCIDENT INVESTIGATION
METHODOLOGIES, BOTH MILITARY AND CIVILIAN 7

CHAPTER 3: COGNITION, AERONAUTICAL DECISION
MAKING AND SITUATIONAL AWARENESS 23

CHAPTER 4: ADVANCEMENT OF AERONAUTICS
AND SAFETY INFORMATION SHARING 41

CHAPTER 5: A-7 CORSAIR GENERAL, EMERGENCY
AND EJECTION SEAT 49

CHAPTER 6: SUGGESTED REMEDIATIONS 55

CHAPTER 7: 10 SOULS 65

EPILOGUE 71

ADDITIONAL RESOURCES 79

ENDNOTES 81

ABOUT THE AUTHOR 83

PREFACE

ON OCTOBER 20, 1987, at 9:17am, a propulsion-less and pilotless US Air Force A-7D Corsair Attack Aircraft crashed into a Ramada Inn near Indianapolis International Airport. Nine hotel employees and one hotel visitor were killed as a result of the aircraft's impact and instantaneous combustion of 6500 pounds of JP-4 jet fuel. Eight minutes earlier, the Corsair was being piloted by Major Bruce L. Teagarden of the 4450th Tactical Air Wing, out of Nellis Air Force Base, Nevada, when the aircraft's single jet engine malfunctioned and flamed out at 31,000 feet.[1]

Of the ten victims lost as a result of the crash that day, although it took seven additional days for the only non-employee victim to die from burns over 95% of his body, four were burned beyond recognition and five died from smoke inhalation. Some of the victims had higher levels of carbon monoxide, suggesting that these victims survived for some measure of time after the initial impact.[2]

Because of the Air Traffic Control (ATC) mayday alert, Indianapolis International Airport Fire Department arrived at the Ramada Inn within one minute of the aircraft's impact and began fire suppression and rescue operations. Also responding to the scene were Wayne Township and Decatur Township Fire Departments. Before striking the Ramada Inn, the jet struck the roof of a bank building across the street. With its ruptured fuel tanks, and enough energy to keep it flying, it literally crashed through the front door. The impact caused separation of the cockpit and engine from the wings and fuselage. These two components came to rest in the front lobby while the wings and fuselage ended up just above the carport.

Firefighters and EMT's entered the west end of the building looking for victims. Additionally, firefighters and EMT's treated a Ramada employee who had exited the building through an east end door. One of the victims told rescuers that there were more people alive and trapped in the hotel laundry room. Even though the main fire was extinguished within three minutes, firefighters were precluded, by order of the fire chief, from search and rescue of any victims until a determination of aircraft armaments could be made. Twenty-five minutes into the disaster, the fire was essentially suppressed.

Within seconds of the engine failure at 31,000 feet, the A-7 entered the clouds. Major Teagarden notified ATC of the situation and requested assistance. Although the A-7's main power source was disabled, the aircraft had electrical and hydraulic functions that redundant emergency equipment within the aircraft allowed primary control capabilities during an engine failure. The ram air turbine (RAT) extends from the right side of the fuselage into the slip stream. The slip stream rotates a small turbine at several thousand revolutions per minute (RPMs). The turbine then turns a generator, providing auxiliary power. During his decent, Major Teagarden tried fourteen to seventeen times to restart the engine. Each restart attempt took precious time and altitude away from the aircraft remaining aloft. In fact, because the requirements for

PREFACE

successful re-start, in part, include the engine wind milling at twelve percent RPM, the aircraft glide speed has to be increased to 270 knots for that to happen. This higher-than-normal glide speed, in turn, reduces the best glide range of the aircraft by ten percent. In other words, the aircraft would glide about forty-five nautical miles from an altitude of 31,000 feet while the pilot tries to restart the engine. It's worth noting that there are numerous large bodies of water, thousands of acres of farmland, and the White River within forty-five miles of where the Corsair's engine quit.

ATC, responding to Major Teagarden's declaration of mayday, informed him of the nearest Air Force Base to his position, Terre Haute, IN at forty-four miles. They then asked Major Teagarden if that's where he wanted to proceed, to which he replied affirmative. ATC provided Major Teagarden with radar vectors to Terre Haute and asked him if he would be able to accept a "turn away" from the airport because of traffic. Major Teagarden responded that he was unable to accept that request because he had to get on the ground. ATC then asked if he would prefer to try and land at Indianapolis International Airport that was located fifteen miles to the north of his current position. Major Teagarden accepted ATC's suggestion and provided him with vectors to the airport. By this time, the A-7 was at an altitude of 12,000 feet and descending at 3500 feet per minute. At six minutes into the emergency, Major Teagarden asks ATC if there are any housing areas that are close to his position in case he had to eject himself from the aircraft. The City of Indianapolis had a population of approximately 750,000, in 1987.

Ten seconds later, Major Teagarden again asked ATC about any housing areas. By this time, ATC advised Major Teagarden to expect a "straight in" approach to runway four left and that his A-7 was four miles from the airport. ATC continued to provide Major Teagarden position reports as the aircraft got closer to the runway. It must be pointed out that as the aircraft got closer to the runway, Major Teagarden could not see the ground or the airport environment because of the overcast conditions. This lack of visual contact prevented any ability to correct the aircraft's glide angle or of establishing the proper airport pattern altitude. Not surprisingly, the A-7, still at 3100 feet, overflew the runway. ATC then instructed Major Teagarden to turn right and set up for an approach to runway thirty-one. It was during this right turn that Major Teagarden was able to make visual contact with the ground.

Major Teagarden, as instructed by ATC, began a right turn for runway thirty-one. It was during the turn that Major Teagarden realized he could not make the runway. In a statement, made afterwards to the press, Major Teagarden said he was coming down in a housing area, so he aimed the A-7 at an open field and ejected. However, the force from the ejection seat propulsion system disrupted the A-7's course and attitude (aircraft attitude is defined as: straight and level, turning or bank, ascending and descending) from that set by Major Teagarden before he bailed out. As Major Teagarden parachuted to an assured certain safety, he landed in the parking lot of the Ace Supply Company. Workers inside came out to check on the pilot. Other than some minor abrasions, Major Teagarden was in good condition. Major Teagarden immediately asked one of the Ace Supply workers to use a telephone. The first person he called was his wife. He then called his command center and according to an Ace Supply worker, Major Teagarden talked, albeit softly, for quite some time.

PREFACE

By the time Major Teagarden finished talking on the phone, a county deputy sheriff arrived and drove him to the hospital. It wasn't until Major Teagarden was asked by an official while being treated at the hospital did emergency responders know whether the jet fighter contained any armaments.

On the morning of October 20, 1987, Air Force Major Teagarden flew his A-7 Corsair attack jet aircraft out of Pittsburgh International Airport. Three days earlier he flew to Pittsburgh from USAF base in Nevada. The trip was authorized by the Air Force as an instrument proficiency flight. However, the pilot used the convenience to attend a funeral of a fellow airman, Gary Swisher, in Mannington, West Virginia, and to visit with family in Pennsylvania.

That same morning, 300 miles to the southwest of Pittsburgh, a Ramada Inn started it's day with most of the hotel's guest checking out. Thankfully, the timing of the crash prevented potentially many more casualties then had occurred.

The subsequent chapters have been formulated to provide an in-depth cross section of information relating to the pilot, the aircraft, safety protocols, politics, litigation, human physiology, accident investigations (civilian and military), suggested remediations, situational awareness, aeronautical decision making, and the importance of safety information sharing. Lastly, and most importantly, I will present a personal look into the lives of the victims. The victims were Emma Jean Brownlee, Ruth Katherine Cox, Christopher L. Evans, Beth Goldberg, Brenda J. Henry, Narinder S. Kanwar, Allen Dale Mantor, Mary Stuart Marsh, Dawn Shelly Martin, and Thomas C. Murray.

1

THE UN-SILENT KNIGHT

ALAN E. DIEHL, PH.D. is a former Senior USAF Safety Scientist and a prolific author of aviation safety publications. His career focus has been a multi-decade long concentration of the aeronautical decision making and crew resource managements (CRM) disciplines. Alan was drawn to his career at an early age, having grown up on military bases named after dead heroes. He soon learned that safety was rarely a top priority for military leaders. Because of this cavalier safety attitude, Alan set his sight and future career on doing something to bring meaningful change to this pervasive affliction. Alan, just as in this author's pursuit, always wants to keep the wellbeing of the victims' families front and center. These families have suffered much too long not knowing the truth of why they lost loved ones.

The following pages of this chapter and subsequent chapter, in part, have been taken from Alan's 2002 book, "Silent Knights." The reproduction of which has Alan's complete and full permission. It is done so based on Alan's own words (to this author), "You are doing the right thing," as its guide.

Institutionalized Abuses:
"This corrupt system operates with impunity because of several factors. Moreover, it has operated like this for decades-unchallenged.

As such, it has become the perfect manifestation of how absolute power corrupts absolutely. It simply has no effective checks and balances. Leaders are not above the law-they are the law. Furthermore, they like it that way.

They are simply not held accountable for their safety decisions. A senior Pentagon official once told me, "We don't need independent investigations because we own the equipment and the people." I respectfully disagreed by reminding him that the equipment belonged to the taxpayers and that the American people had entrusted us to safeguard their loved ones. I also noted that our troops have no union to protect them, only our sense of integrity.

The civilian world has a legally mandated system of checks and balances, which involves well-established "fire walls" between critical decisions. In the U.S. aviation, for instance, the operator (commercial airlines), the investigative (National Transportation Safety Board), and the regulators (Federal Aviation Administration) are separate and totally independent from one another.

But in the military, these functions are merged into one all-powerful organization. The operators (major command), the investigators (safety centers), and the regulators (Defense Department), are all a part of the same monolithic organization. Moreover, an impenetrable wall of secrecy surrounds this cluster of functioning.

Perhaps the biggest problem in making meaningful reforms, is the sheer size of the military establishment. The critical role that the defense establishment has played to protect the republic's vital interests is actually part of the problem. Most of our institutions – including Congress, presidential administrations, and the court seem very comfortable with the status quo, or they are at least reluctant to confront this behemoth. Critics of the military are frequently viewed as being unpatriotic.

Privilege, as discussed earlier, represent another barrier to improving safety. This concept permits the military to conduct two separate investigations. The first, called the safety investigation, is designed to establish why the accident occurred and hopefully prevent further reoccurrences. This is an "internal use only" document. The second, the accident investigative is a legalistic exercise designed only to establish who is to be blamed for the crash. The later report is, of course, public domain and is intended to placate criticism.

The reader should keep in mind that the military's accident investigation report of the October 20, 1987 crash obtained via FOIA, summed up the cause (blame) as engine failure. The report did not include the pilot's actions, or lack thereof, as totally contributory factors after engine failure. As Alan has so succinctly explained, this aforementioned would be contained in the nonpublic safety report.

The military contends the concept of executive privilege permits results of its safety inquiries to be "secret." Of course, because the information normally has nothing to do with national security, they have to do some very creative thinking to justify *releasing* the contents of such investigations. Their specious logic contends they have "covenant" with their employees not to reveal the most important information contained in the safety report.

This bogus argument holds that Congress, who authorized the funding for the service, has no right to know why the accident occurred. Likewise, the taxpayers who paid for this equipment, personnel, and operations have no right to know why the accident occurred. Most ludicrous, this logic must hold that the next of kin also should be denied the right to know why their loved one died....

Beneath Human Error:
"Pilot error" is often singled out as *the* cause of aviation disasters. In fact, most statistical studies conclude that crew or operator error is the most common cause of accidents. Typically, between 60 and 90 percent of all accidents are blamed on human error, but safety experts have long noted such conclusions are often the by-product of superficial investigations.

... Sophisticated investigation, by contrast, know that most mishaps do not occur because of a single failure, be it human or material. Rather, there is a deadly "chain of events,' usually a series of seemingly minor problems or deficiencies that cascade in a particular situation to precipitate the accident.

This phenomenon is called the "chain" because if any one of the links is removed, the chain is broken-and the accident does not occur. Typically, the operator is merely the last link in a long sequence of events. Thus, he or she usually just represents the final chance of disrupting the accident chain. The operator's chronological proximity to the accident event often leads to the de facto assignment of blame.

Many underlying factors obviously contribute to crashes, but military safety investigations are particularly fond of citing "pilot error" as the cause of the mishaps, especially when the pilot is dead. This practice institutionalizes the egregious process by literally adding insult to injury.

But on rare occasions, the truth will out. This happens only when members of the investigation have the insight, patience, and courage to expose *all* the factors that contributed to the accident. By doing so, they are refusing to stop at merely identifying *what* has happened and are endeavoring to explain *why* the crash occurred.

Such investigators are willing to uncover the truth no matter where it lies. They simply keep digging until they have uncovered the underlying causes. They often find that, besides the crew performance, several other problems, such as the machine's design, management decisions, and environmental conditions, also played a role in the accident chain.

But more often than not, when one gets to the core of the matter, the "system" is the underlying culprit. The investigative process is not unlike peeling back the layers of an onion. By digging deeper and deeper, one gets at the truth. . . Often, the deeper one digs, the uglier the truth, and most military investigations simply cannot handle the truth."[1]

2
AVIATION ACCIDENT INVESTIGATION METHODOLOGIES, BOTH MILITARY AND CIVILIAN

THIS CHAPTER CONTAINS a substantial descriptive account of the military's accident investigative techniques and a comparative explanation that separates the military from its civilian counterparts, National Transportation Safety Board (NTSB) and the Federal Aviation Administration (FAA).

The military system for mishap investigation involves two separate investigations. The first investigation (both are conducted in parallel) is labeled the safety investigation or SIB. The purpose of the SIB is to establish why the accident occurred and to prevent such future events. The SIB is an "internal use only" report that is never revealed to outside scrutiny.

The second report, titled the accident investigation report or AIB, is designed to place blame on the cause of the mishap. The AIB, of course, is public domain, intended to pacify criticism. Examples of AIB's tend to contain fair amounts of similarities across hundreds that were reviewed for this publication. These can be broken down into the following general and generic categories:

- Date, time and location of mishap
- Name and rank of personnel directly involved
- Home base of mishap personnel

- Location (home base) of the accident investigative board personnel
- Synopsis of the event
- Findings (accident sequence)
- Diagram of the scene/impact area
- Photos of the scene/impact area

A glaring omission, even for the lay person, is information taken from witnesses. Whether the military knows it or not, by privileging investigative information, they make victims of those who may have caused the accident. Victims are given immunity. Also missing, although contained in a select few reports, are ATC transcripts. While the discussion of what's contained in an AIB is being bantered about, perhaps it is worth noting that of the eight aforementioned categories listed, only three really carry any significance in determining probable cause of a mishap from a military perspective. Most investigative teams, military and civilian alike, know that the best way to begin an investigation is to work backwards from the moment (time) of the accident. Accordingly, the first phase of the examination should be directed at the unsafe actions taken by the pilot(s), that ultimately led to the accident. It is here, in this domain, that the common refrain of "pilot error" is branded. Afterall, and not unlike a murder investigation, this is where the proverbial "smoking gun" is likely to be found. Typically, at least from a military perspective, this is the area referred to as the Findings Regiment or Accident Sequence. Causes are interspersed throughout several broad, chronological steps or timeline segments that are prepared from the moment before, all the way through impact.

AVIATION ACCIDENT INVESTIGATION METHODOLOGIES

The Navy conducts their investigation similar to the Air Force but, instead of labeling their reports SIB and AIB, the Navy simply calls these reports as part A (non-privileged data)[1] and part B (privilege). The Navy abridges their reports with the following:

FOR OFFICIAL USE ONLY

THIS IS A PRIVILEDGED, LIMITED USE, LIMITED-DISTRIBUTION, SAFETY INVESTIGATION REPORT. UNAUTHORIZED DISCLOSURE OF THE INFORMATION IN THIS REPORT OR ITS SUPPORTING ENCLOSURES BY MILTARY PERSONNEL IS A CRIMINAL OFFENSE PUNISHABLE UNDER ARTICLE 92, UNIFORM CODE OF MILITARY JUSTICE. UNAUTHORIZED DISCLOSURE OF THE INFORMATION IN THIS REPORT OR ITS SUPPORING ENCLOSURES BY CIVILIAN PERSONNEL WILL SUBJECT THEM TO DISCIPLINARY ACTION PURSUANT TO CIVILIAN PERSONNEL INSTRUCTION 752. THIS REPORT MAY NOT BE RELEASED, IN WHOLE OR IN PART, EXCEPT BY THE COMMANDER OF THE NAVAL SAFTEY CENTER.

The military refers to privilege information as a concept. The noun, concept, is defined as a general notion or idea. Some synonyms are consideration, apprehension, supposition, conception, hypothesis, impression, and perception, hardly words that convey a sense of exactness that one would expect in this realm. The military and federal courts grant protection under executive privilege to information given under promises of confidentiality.

(See Freedom of Information Act, (FOIA) Title 5 USC). These two operative words, concept and promises are quite remarkable, especially considering the structured environment surrounding, or at least should be surrounding, an official accident investigation.

As referenced above, the U.S. Military (DOD) conducts two accident investigations for the same event and issues two distinctly different reports. The accident report, which is permitted in the public domain, is crafted for the sole purpose of establishing who or what is to blame for the accident. The second referred to as the safety report, is cloaked in a protected legislated vail.

The legislated protection affords the military from public disclosure of important accident information. Title 5, USC Part 552 protects the release of information by sheltering it under the guise of privilege. Pursuant to the referenced statute, privileged information includes statements, reports or testimony given to safety investigators or boards under the promises of confidentiality, and any direct reference to any such statements or testimony elsewhere in a report. The findings, evaluations, analysis, opinions, conclusions, recommendations and other indicia of the deliberative processes of safety investigations, safety investigative boards, endorsers and reviewers are also privileged safety information. It must be so noted that the information categorized as privileged **is precisely the information that would provide victim survivors the closure they desperately deserve**. Just as important is this currently clandestine information's promising effect on aviation safety throughout the entire aviation industry, military and civilian alike. Antidotally, an example of the many challenges that invalidates the privileged persuasion is "testimonial immunity." However, the transformation, if there is going to be one, will ultimately require congressional interest, through legislation, to amend Title 5 USC, Part 552. In the interim, challenges from investigative researchers must continue to come forward. Accordingly, it is with the sincerest intent of this author to provide the surviving families of the events of October 20, 1987 with sufficient information to finally find that elusive closure.

AVIATION INVESTIGATIONS

Methods of investigative techniques (Ludwig Benner Jr.)

1. There are over 30 investigative methods used by practitioners. However, a common thread to these methods is overarching. Criminal prosecution, questions of guilt for the purpose of laying blame and the prevention of future accidents form the core to all these methodologies.

2. Determination, regarding the cause of an accident or mishap, is a psychological (social) rather that a logical or rational process. The cause of the accident, using this mindset, is that the cause is never found, but instead constructed. (Hollande, 2015)

3. Contemporary research to understanding accidents and mishaps seems to focus on the use of reports and case studies instead of empirical observation of what lead to the conclusion of how it was produced. To state it another way, did the description of events and

assertions contain a mix of empirical data and the investigators own created judgement? Allowing perceptual biases and or motivational incentives cloud and affect the reported data.

4. Evaluating investigative methods, and their comparative merits, differ wildly and have consequences. This is manifested because of differing views and becomes handicapped by the latitude investigators are provided with when reporting data. Rational investigations prevent similar mishaps and they also identify and mitigate against perpetuation of process inefficiencies and wasted resources.

What can be done to help effect credible prevention strategies (I.J. Rimson)

1. There needs to be an effort to erase artificial distinctions between "government safety investigators" and the rest of the community. All air safety investigators, whether they represent government, manufacturers, airlines, airline employee unions, or insurers should be held to the same objectives, methodologies and procedures which can withstand critical scrutiny.

2. Criteria must be established that defines what an Air Safety Investigator (ASI) is and does. A qualified ASI should be trained, experienced and have the cognitive ability to remain objective.

3. A conscious effect must be made to publicly expose agencies and persons responsible for obstructing accident prevention.

4. Those effected should be willing to oppose politically-inspired dissipation of investigative assets into areas beyond the missions and capabilities of investigative professionals. Above all, the leaders of U.S. government investigative agencies should be encouraged to cooperate with the rest of the world's investigators.

Investigating Investigation Methodologies (Ludwig Benner, Jr.)

Multilinear Events Sequencing (MES) based investigation methodology is used by the NTSB. MES is a self-directing, rule-oriented investigation methodology, derived from observation of and experimentation with investigation processes. MES does not use causes. Instead, it focuses on specific behaviors and interactions that need to be changed to improve positive outcomes. MES tries to identify interactions that should not occur, or should occur differently, to affect positive change.

Ludwig Benner, Jr. rated accident models and investigation methodologies in the Journal of Safety Research. (vol. 16, pp 105-126, 1985 Ludwig Benner, Jr.) Benner references methodologies used by seventeen government accident investigative departments. Each agency's model or method used is ranked on its effectiveness to produce reasoned accident causation and provide recommendation for mitigation of future events. For example, OSHA (DOL field manual 1982) used a violation model. Violating a standard could cause an accident (lowest ranked). The highest ranked methodology would be expected to turn better results even after years had elapsed since the original investigation.

Alan Diehl, a former USAF Safety Scientist, separates "pilot error" from "human error."

Pilot error involves discretion. It occurs when a pilot purposefully, or knowingly violates rules or procedures. Human error occurs as the result from human imperfection.

Military investigative methodologies are the exception rather than the rule. The military is indeed privileged and therefore protected by the military U.S. Code, Part 5. Safety information that can and should be made available with all categories of aviation, civilian and military alike, is not "shared." More specific, information on military accident investigative procedures is described in chapter 3.

The National Transportation Safety Board (NTSB) and the Federal Aviation Administration (FAA) are the civilian aviation agencies tasked with the responsibilities for accident investigations and aviation safety. Their mandate includes all civilian aviation activities which includes general aviation and the airlines.

There are acute differences, however, in these two agencies, but they are brought together with a common goal. Aviation safety drives these two agencies in no uncertain terms even though they are separate and distinct. However, many variables affect true empirical problem solving, and solutions and safety recommendations because of decades long agency culture. These barriers are discussed in greater detail below. The NTSB Mission Statement has been duplicated as follows:

AVIATION ACCIDENT INVESTIGATION METHODOLOGIES

The National Transportation Safety Board is an independent Federal agency charged by Congress with investigating every civil aviation accident in the United States and significant accidents in other modes of transportation – railroad, highway, marine and pipeline. The NTSB determines the probable cause of the accidents and issues safety recommendations aimed at preventing future accidents. In addition, the NTSB carries out special studies concerning transportation safety and coordinates the resources of the Federal Government and other organizations to provide assistance to victims and their family members impacted by major transportation disasters.

- Maintaining our congressionally mandated independence and objectivity
- Conducting objective, precise accident investigations and safety studies
- Performing fair and objective airman and mariner certification appeals
- Advocating and promoting safety recommendation
- Assisting victims of transportation accidents and their families

IMPROVING AVIATION ACCIDENT REPORTS

Putting aside the notion of the military's nondisclosure protection provided by legislation, if and when their privileged reports can be opened to the public domain, these reports will require change. The military must adopt a heuristic model using modus ponens (method of affirming cause) and modus tollens (mode that by denying, denies) characteristics used by accident investigators. Unless witnesses have the opportunity to comment on an investigator's treatment of their evidence, then the public domain can have little confidence that important contextual information has not been omitted or improperly summarized. Further, analysis must be presented at a level which supports the report's findings and enables the improvement of future operational, system, and managerial changes for safety improvements.

"If "probable cause" is ok for safety, it certainly is unsatisfactory for prevention and entirely unacceptable for investigations. Who wants to pay for an investigation whose result is "probable cause" except someone who doesn't want to know for sure, anyhow?" (Hughes Chicoine). Aviation accident investigators are in a cynical business. They seek only human imperfection.

The "probable cause" nomenclature has been historically rooted. The 1934 Amendment to the 1926 Air Commerce Act became the standard and is still in use today. The military has been able to get away with even more nebulous terms such as "possible cause." As with the military's duplicitous investigative practices provided by congressional legislation, the NTSB has also a share in the scapegoating of abysmal investigative practices. It allows both entities to produce an intended equivocation of empirical facts, does nothing with respect to prevention and safety. The NTSB's legislative mandate, gleaned from their website, reads in part: Charged by congress with investigating all civil aviation accidents in the U.S., the NTSB determines the probable cause of the accidents. Therefore, and with respect to the deadly incident of Indianapolis, the cause and effect investigative model will be used.

AVIATION ACCIDENT INVESTIGATION METHODOLOGIES

The cause equals effect investigative model can withstand vulnerability to special interest (which may include their own organizations). It is a difficult and quite nearly impossible to massage and apple into an orange with the use of this investigative methodology! Although influence from special interest has been prevented from seeping into any part of the decision to publish this author's efforts, at the same time making a presentation less complicated does work best because it is done so with more freedom of truthful expression.

Background, to the cause equals effect, has been provided for the reader to readily grasp. Simply put, if cause **A** will result in effect **B**, then the absence of cause **A** will result in the absence of effect **B**. As the logic and application of this model is used for the October 20, 1987 accident, the causes will be brought forth in narrative format and preceded with (**C**). Similarly, the effect will be presented also in narrative format and preceded with (**E**). The reader will then have the subjective information from which to draw their own conclusions.

(**C**) There was a failure of the aircraft engine high speed gearbox drive mechanism. This failure prevented fuel supply, air mixture, and ignition to the engine resulting in complete engine failure. (**E**) A powerless aircraft was incapable of maintaining a sustained cruising flight. (**C**) The cockpit engine revolutions per minute (RPM) gauge, which went to zero RPM's when engine failure occurred, would require a 15% RPM value for the pilot to attempt an engine restart. In order for the engine to produce 15% RPM, using the slipstream, the aircraft airspeed must have had to be increased to produce the requisite RPM. This would require increasing the glide speed, thereby decreasing the glide distance and time the aircraft could remain aloft. **(E)** Human perseveration, or plan continuation bias (error) took over the pilot's cognitive capabilities and thought processes. The bias stigmatized the pilot's actions at a time when all informational options required consideration. The pilot continued with multiple (14-17) futile attempts to restart the engine.

(C) The regional weather, including Indianapolis, precluded a visual operating environment for arriving and departing aircraft. All operations had to be conducted under instrument flight rules (IFR). IFR conditions are defined as a cloud ceiling of less than one thousand feet above ground level (AGL) and/or visibility of less than three statute miles. Indianapolis weather, at the time of the accident, was an eight-hundred-foot ceiling and five miles visibility. In essence, the weather prevented the pilot from using visual cues required to make a successful emergency landing. The weather conditions cannot be underestimated because it made the landing attempt nearly impossible and most certainly 99.9% improbable. **(E)** The pilot's plan continuation bias stigmatized his proper resolve to follow Air Force (AF) emergency operating procedures (EOP). AF EOP's forbids pilots from attempting an engine-out landing attempt in a heavily populated area. The EOP also forbids pilots from attempting an engine-out landing attempt in instrument meteorological conditions. The operative wording in the EOP's section of the manual is *shall not* be made if these conditions are present.

It is blatantly clear the reasoning behind these engine-out prohibitions. Unfortunately, they become manifested in real-time and were sadly realized on 10/20/1987. **(C)** Air traffic control (ATC) suggests to the pilot that Terra Haute, Indiana Airport has Air National Guard Station located there and asks the pilot if he would like radar vectors to that location. The pilot replied affirmative, but after realizing the distance to Terra Haute asks ATC for a closer location. ATC advises the pilot that Indianapolis International Airport (IND) would be closer and provides the pilot with radar vectors to IND. The pilot asked ATC if there were houses located near the airport because he said that he might have to "get out of this thing." The pilot's reference to getting out of this thing is in direct reference to the use of the ejection seat. **(E)** The jet was powerless except of auxiliary electrical and hydraulic capabilities. The plane was completely obscured by clouds, yet continues descent towards the airport. The pilot continues to perform the airborne engine restart sequences. He attempted to restart the engine 14-17 times. Again, all of the actions and lack of actions are brutally in opposition to EOP. The pilot did not think to jettison fuel to mitigate a post-crash inferno.

(C) The weather, as referenced previously, prevented the visual cues required to make a successful emergency landing. The aircraft was equipped with various redundancies that allow the pilot, when in visual conditions, to adjust the altitude. The pilot can accelerate or retard descent as required to meet the correct glide configuration for an emergency landing. However, without visual conditions that becomes an impossible task. **(E)** Indianapolis ATC informed the pilot to expect an engine-out approach to landing on runway 040 left. ATC, knowing that the emergency aircraft is a military attack airplane, never asked the pilot if the aircraft was carrying armaments. Conversely, the pilot didn't offer this information either. *Military aircraft carry live ordnances in only limited situations when flying in U.S. Airspace. An* example of this is when the aircraft is assigned to national security readiness details. Otherwise, stateside flying operations are done without armaments.

(C) The aircraft arrived over IND with too high an altitude and lacked the visual contact to attempt the landing on runway 040 left. **(E)** ATC instructed the pilot to make a right turn and advise when he had visual contact that he could attempt a landing on runway 310. **(C)** The pilot initiated a right turn for runway 310, and during the turn he finally descended below the overcast. He advised ATC that he may have to "get out of this thing" (eject) because he was going down in a housing area. **(E)** The pilot decided to deploy the ejection seat. He egressed from the aircraft and parachuted to safety.

(C) The pilotless aircraft, in the landing configuration (wheels extended), with nearly full fuel tanks and no armaments was heading into a populated area. **(E)** The aircraft struck a flat roofed (then) Bank One building. The velocity and corresponding energy released after striking the building, caused the fuel tanks to rupture. The aircraft, spewing JP-4 jet fuel, then lurched into a Ramada Inn Hotel directly through the front door lobby area and a post collision fire ensued.

(C) First responders, fire and rescue arrived on the scene immediately. They extinguished the post-crash fire within a minute's time. However, the fire chief prevented his rescue team from entering the scene and begin search and rescue because it wasn't known whether the aircraft was carrying armaments. The pilot, who parachuted to safety in a parking lot located a very short distance from the accident site was indifferent and did not engage with first responders at the scene. Instead, the pilot used the phone at the Acme Company to call his wife and his commanding officer. After the calls, a deputy sheriff takes him to the hospital. The fire chief did not get his answer concerning the aircraft armament until almost an hour later. (**E**) The nine employees of the hotel and one casual visitor perished as the result of the crash. Four employees were burned beyond recognition and required forensic science for identification. Five employees died from smoke inhalation. They all had high levels of carbon monoxide, that measured from 4.1 percent to 76.8 percent. The employees with the highest levels, according to the medical examiner, were alive for "some time" after the jet crashed and the fire flared. However, because of the lack of armament information, search and rescue had been delayed. The hotel's casual visitor sustained severe burns over 95 percent of his body before ultimately perishing several days later.

3
COGNITION, AERONAUTICAL DECISION MAKING AND SITUATIONAL AWARENESS

PILOTING AN AIRCRAFT requires more cognition skills than just about any human endeavor. Flying an aircraft presents one of the greatest challenges to the cognitive capabilities of humans, in large part because it involves the control of a vehicle that defies the natural forces of gravity. From a cognitive psychology standpoint, the task of flying should be considered from three different perspectives. The first is cognitive analysis (preflight planning for weather and other enroute purposes), describes the different tasks a pilot must carry out. The second are the physical characteristics of aircraft systems (aircraft inspection and mechanical condition), which are the focus of the pilot's tasks. The third represents pilot information (pooling of all resources and bringing them together), processing structures, in different combinations, that accomplish those tasks.

The aircraft is a dynamic system that depends upon the operator processing an accurate mental model of the systems to establish expectancies of their response to environmental and control input. Pilots control the attitude of the aircraft by adjusting for pitch, bank and yaw. In short, pilots must be able to multitask.

There are many cognitive errors a pilot might fall victim to. The first one is called black/white thinking. This thinking error, also known as cognitive distortion, is "all or none thinking." It's my way, or the highway, type thinking. Anytime we believe there are no other options that are available, we create confusion and chaos. We can get in trouble very quickly! This type of thinking causes us to think narrow mindedly. Cognitive distortion is an enemy to open communication, humility, and give and take interactions. As has been described (Arkes and Hammond 1986), a salient feature of decision making is uncertainty. The source of this uncertainty can stem from unreliable information cues. For example, a pilot who experienced an engine failure may get instrument cues that an "air start" is possible, when in fact it isn't, because of internal engine damage. This creates an illusory correlation that further distorts judgement and cognitive decision making (Chapman 1967). There is a strong propensity for humans to seek confirmatory evidence rather than disconformity evidence (Nickerson 1998). As an example, in aviation there is a phrase or term referred to as the "critical triangle of agreement." Essentially, if two sides of the triangle are in agreement and opposed to one side in disagreement, then the purpose of agreement has been achieved.

Hope is on the horizon, in what appears, at least, from an apparent trend that has been initiated by the U.S. Navy/Marine Corps. These military branches have realized the importance of expanding their mishap domain to include human factor considerations. In the 1980's, the Navy was confronted with problems whose roots were imbedded within the culture and tradition of their organization. Mishap occurrences, brought on by bending the rules, were increasing. The Navy referred to this phenomenon as "flexibility." Let's face it, for nearly two centuries, the Navy had empowered their front-line warriors with the ability to make tactical decisions on their own. You live by the sword or die by the sword. In other words, you live by your decision or perish. In a purely tactical environment, you either kill or be killed. It's as simple as that. Any second guessing in combat can be fatal and therefor not an option.

Accordingly, a couple of persons of distinguished merit and ability in the science of human factors psychology (remember, the Navy realized it had a problem), were convinced that their Human Factors Analysis and Classification System, HFACS, could prove useful from an interventional perspective. Drs. Douglas A. Wiegmann and Scott A. Shappell took their program to the US Navy and remarkable positive results followed. Specifically, and for similar, paralleling purposes of this book, Wiegmann and Shappell applied HFACS to Naval accidents which occurred as a result of rules and regulation violations. Overall accident rates are dependent on many variables. However, HFACS allowed its monitors to be selective to specific types of human errors. In a three-year period, between 1997-2000, using HFACS intervention principles, the U.S. Navy/Marine Corps accidents associated with rules and regulations violations dropped off precipitously.

Before delving into the nuts and bolts of Wiegmann's and Shappell's HFACS model, these human factors psychologists built their program's foundation, in part, upon the building blocks laid previously by James Reason. Dr. Reason's work reference, herein, is in no way meant to diminish others in the field that have contributed immensely, but, as those others would probably agree, no one has had the impact in such universal manner as the Reason model of accident causation. Dr. Reason's model was originally developed for the nuclear power industry. The Reason model of accident causation is based on fundamental elements that are germane to all successful organizations. That is, successful organizations are able to harmonize their operations into an efficient and safe exchange of responsibilities between all relevant participants. The N result, according to Dr. Reason, is consistently unblemished and seamless product or service conceived and ultimately motivated to carry out its mission throughout a safe environment.

Hyperbole aside, the Reason thesis was conceived by taking a complicated area of human psychology and turning it into a practical measure or organizational effectiveness. Dr. Reason concluded that before productive activities could occur, certain preconditions needed to exists. Among them were a well-trained and professional workforce and well-maintained equipment. Managers, as part of a well-trained and professional workforce, require support from decision-makers further up the chain-of-command. These same decision makers often have to balance competing priorities and resources enroute to safe, on-time, and cost-effective operation. Obviously, in most organizations, these system elements function very well, however, on occasion, the wheels do come off. Even the most responsible of programs can and do fall prey to the remote probabilities of probabilities.

Dr. Reason proselytized that accidents occur when there were breakdowns of interactions among components within the production of process. These breakdowns or failures diminish the integrity of the system, thereby making it more susceptible to operational hazards, and consequently, to catastrophic failures. Dr. Reason illustrated these failures as "holes" within the different layers of the system. Obviously, the more "holes" or voids within the system layers, a transformation occurs from a productive system into a failed or soon to fail system. By further illustrating the same point, Dr. Reason's theorem resembles a slice of Swiss cheese, hence the name, the Swiss Cheese Model of Accident Causation.

Dr. Reason categorized failures as either latent or active. Latent failures, as the name suggests, may lie dormant for hours, days, weeks, or even months until one day, they cause a catastrophic event on an unsuspecting crew. Latent failures can cause even the best investigators to totally overlook them. Active failures, conversely, represent real-time actions of aircrews such as forgetting to lower the landing gear or flying into bad weather. This is the level where most accident investigators typically focus their attention. We've all seen or heard accident reports that use the common refrain of pilot error. After all, it is these activities or lack of them that can be directly linked to an event or accident.

Returning, for a moment, to the latent failure concept, Dr. Reason described additional levels of human failures that are also a part of the complete inventory when evaluating a system's breakdown. First, there are preconditions to safe-less acts. These preconditions involve such things as mental fatigue, improper communication, or improper communication and or coordination, frequently referred to as crew resource management (CRM). A quick note here regarding CRM, is that it is not restricted to just the crew flying the aircraft, but many involve support personnel external to the flight as you will see later. The second level of failure that contributes to the breakdown of a productive system deals with the ergonomics perspective such as poorly maintained equipment. The third level, which can link the other two levels in accident causation, focuses on instances of unsafe supervision.

It is worth mentioning that Dr. Reason's work did not stop at the supervisory level either. The organization itself can also be culpable in events that lead to human failures. For instance, if two inexperienced pilots are assigned together on a flight into know adverse weather at night, the organization is increasing the possibility of human failure. Service imposed austerity programs contribute to flight time and inexperience. These examples both suggest a lack of supervision. Most assuredly, it makes sense then, that if accidents are going to be reduced, investigators and analysts will have to examine accident sequences in their entirety. Casual, as well as active factors, at all levels within an organization, will have to be addressed if any progress is to be made in accident investigation and prevention. The organizational element, in the overall scheme, is intriguing and will be addressed in greater detail later. For now though, the physiological state of mind and the physical/mental limitations of personnel within a system require due diligence.

Mental preparedness is critical in nearly every life endeavor, but especially so in aviation. An individual's condition, both mentally and physically, can, and often does, influence performance on the job. Whether the job is flying a plane, operating on a patient, or working construction, they all require a high degree of total fitness. Therefore, investigators have appropriately created a category referred to as "mental state." The adverse mental state category, as an investigative consideration, captures information relating to those mental conditions that affect performance. Paramount among these performance issues is the loss of <u>situational awareness, task fixation, distraction, attentional tunneling (perseveration), and mental fatigue</u>

due to sleep loss and or other stressors. Each of these mental conditions, affects performance and deserves to be selectively described to appreciate the full impact on an aviator's ability to perform.

Circadian rhythm describes a physiological process or biological clock in humans on a 25-27-hour cycle. The word circadian is derived from Latin meaning, "circa dies", or about a day. William Shakespeare described this rhythm of sleep as the nectar of life. Furthermore, and in some references, it has been applied to rhythmic biological functions associated with (1) an internal "biologic clock" or endogenous rhythm, (2) the intrinsic sleep vs. wake cycle, and/or, (3) exogenous stimuli like solar day-night cycle, temperature, and social environment to name a few. The importance of the aforementioned solar day-night cycle on human performance, can be fortified by the ultimate passage of the Standard Time Act (adaptation of 4 time zones) of March 19, 1918. Prior to its passage, there were no standard time zones. In fact, there were more that one hundred different time zones throughout the United States. All these time zones were based on "sun" time, in individual towns, determined by the best local estimate of "noon".

The biological aspects of the circadian rhythm are remarkable. From secretions of hormones that arouse the sleeper just before waking, to excretion of spent excessive hormones two hours after the beginning of the cycle. Body temperature decreases to its lowest value, producing a corresponding decrease in blood flow and body metabolism. There is a decrease in amplification and rate of breathing during sleep. In trying to meet some form of semblance to a perspective of understanding the effects of desynchronization of the diurnal rhythm, one should turn to practices that Wiley Post observed.[1] Wiley Post was a famed American aviator who was the first pilot to fly solo around the world, completing the 15,474-mile trip in seven days, nineteen hours, on July 22, 1933. Mr. Post's triumph over circumnavigating the globe can be attributed, in part, to his recognition of the effects of diurnal rhythm on human performance. Mr. Post took this knowledge very seriously by preparing its inevitable effects months in advance. Mr. Post learned how to eat and sleep at irregular times in order to break regular habits. By doing so, he readjusted his biological clock so that his body was out of phase of the first part of his global flight but in phase for the second part of the flight. Many years after Mr. Post's historic flight, the FAA conducted several studies concerning this phenomenon and concluded that it took several days to re-synchronize the biological clock after flights through several time zones. Also, eastward travel causes the body's clock to advance because it shortens or abbreviates a person's day. Therefore, resynchronization is much slower after completing a multiple time zone flight from west to east. As a postscript, Mr. Post was killed, along with his good friend, Will Rogers, in Alaska in 1935 as a result of faulty equipment on the aircraft he was flying.

After an unscheduled landing near Fairbanks, Alaska, because of bad weather, they again resumed their flight. However, soon after lift off the engine failed and both Post and Rogers were killed instantly upon impact.

In continuance of the mental preparedness aspect of human performance on flight, the effects of a certain stressor can have debilitating consequences to an aviator's performance and decision-making capabilities. However, since reaction to events that produce stress are human, it then goes without saying that not all stress is bad stress. Stress keeps you alert and focused, it prevents boredom and promotes vigilance, to name a few.[2] Consequently, though, it is stress saturation that promotes negative human performance characteristics that become problematic.

Decisions and or causes that accident investigators often label as the results of accidents as "probable cause or pilot error", are easy to identify after the fact. It is simplistic, to say the least, what a pilot *could* have done to have averted the 1987 accident. This line of thought suffers from what is known as "hindsight bias." By jumping over or disregarding the importance of cognitive factors of accident causation, an accident investigation becomes a boilerplate with little value to prevention or to remedy future accidents. Therefore, the importance of a cognitive appraisal (Lazarus and Folkman 1984) cannot and must not be omitted from the investigative process. The physiological science bears this out. When an individual begins to experience a life-threatening turn of events during an emergency, the individual starts to question his or her ability to manage the event successfully. As the problem escalates, anxiety begins to override the cognitive process. Attention Control Theory (Allsop and Gray 2014) poses that anxiety disrupts attention management in three ways: (a) It reduces normal control which may include simulated emergency procedures that were practiced in hopes of providing long-term memory. This causes attention to be compromised to less important tasks, (b) As indicated above, when stress induces anxiety, the anxiety impairs the pilot's ability to manage separate, but highly important tasks, and (c) the anxiety causes perseveration or the impulse to continue the same ineffective actions over and over, but expecting successful results.

Team decision making, meaning using outside the cockpit resources, has been proven useful and contributory to problem solving. Air Traffic Control, dispatch, maintenance, and third-party intervention have been proven to be successful at mitigating negative mishap results. This, however requires training between team members, and/or sharing of team member tasks and knowing each other's team contributing strengths and weaknesses. The FAA has sponsored "Operation Raincheck" for decades to assist the aviation community. This allows pilots the chance to see and understand how valuable information sharing can assist pilot/controller interaction, safely, in the entire airspace environment.

The empirical research that correlates stress and cognitive physiology must be defined by identifying the errors that have occurred as they relate to managing or not managing the actions during abnormal events. During the events of October 20, 1987, the following have been clearly documented:

- There was a deliberate failure to follow procedures by deciding to attempt a dead stick landing (inoperative engine) in instrument meteorological conditions (IFR), and allowing a landing attempt in a populated area.

- There was a deliberate failure to follow procedures by attempting a dead-stick landing when High Key (5000 ft. above ground level, AGL) or Low Key (3000 ft. AGL) could not be satisfactorily achieved. These references to

COGNITION, AERONAUTICAL DECISION MAKING AND SITUATIONAL AWARENESS

pattern altitude can only be achieved in visual metrological conditions.

- There was a deliberate failure to follow procedures for the number of attempted engine air-starts. Air Force procedures instruct pilots to take alternative action after several failed engine air-start attempts have proved futile. Had the pilot followed proper procedures, it would have provided ample time to jettison fuel to prevent a post-crash fire. Additionally, alternative actions would have provided the pilot the thought process of further abnormal situational activities such as an off-airport landing, ditching, and (ATC) requested vectors to suitable, rural airport facilities.

- There was a failure to engage outside the cockpit team coordination. Air Traffic Control (ATC) and Air Force maintenance specialist at Terre Haute could have provided valuable assistance in mitigating some high-risk elements of the event had they been using team member capacities.

- There was a failure to maintain situational awareness or the ability to know the aircraft position in relationship to ground references, instrument landing systems (ILS), populated areas, rural areas, and bodies of water. Situational awareness must be maintained regardless of visual flight rules or instrument flight rules. It should be noted there that in the referenced event, the pilot asked

33

ATC if Indianapolis was a populated area. However, the fact that Indianapolis was indeed a heavily populated metropolitan city did not influence his preordained decision to eject from the powerless aircraft.

- The deliberate failure to following procedures and the attributable anxiety produced by the threat to the pilot's well-being, quickly evaporated the cognitive ability to manage the outcome of the event successfully.

The following errors/events have been documented, as fact, when the pilot continued the following activities. It must be noted that these transgressions, although factual, only infer the neurological pathology previously referenced. They have been provided for the sole purpose of realistic, but not factual evaluation. The survivors and curious readers must come to their own summation of the events of 10/20/1987. Accordingly, the following has been provided:

- Because of the deliberate failure to follow procedures by attempting a dead-stick landing in instrument meteorological conditions, the pilot, after receiving ATC vectors to the Indianapolis runway, overflew the runway by 3000 feet. This occurred because the recorded ceiling, or the base of the overcast, was 800 feet above ground level. There a number of actions a pilot can take to make the aircraft quickly lose altitude, but only if the pilot had visual contact with the airport.

- Because the pilot overshot the intended runway, ATC provided vectors for an alternate runway. By attempting an approach to the alternate runway, the powerless aircraft broke out of the low overcast approximately 800 feet above ground level.

- In the abnormal situation induced disruption to cognitive thinking, and gripped with believing no other options were available, the pilot activated the ejection seat.

- The pilot claimed to have maneuvered the aircraft, before ejecting, to an open unpopulated area. Hower, the aircraft's stability was compromised upon activation of the rocket propelled ejection seat and the corresponding change of aircraft center of gravity (CG).

Situational awareness, or the skill of knowing the aircraft's position or state in a relation to various environmental and geographical dimensions, is the foundation of both visual and instrument flying. There are two properties that formulate accurate situational awareness and the correspondingly critically maintenance of aircraft position referenced by Christopher D. Wickens, Professor of Aviation Human Factors, University of Illinois. Situational awareness involves blending of the cognitive process of perception and working memory. Scientifically, working memory, a temporary storage of information is practicable, but also very vulnerable to proper execution. As an example, pilots might anticipate a certain ATC command, or may not, because they have or have not created a mental picture of the current airspace and the aircraft's actual position.

Situational awareness further includes what is refereed to as "long-term working memory". This element of information, while not actively rehearsed, can be rapidly retrieved if needed. With the combination of these two properties, effective aeronautical decision making, such as whether to continue multiple failed attempts to re-start a disabled engine, as opposed to how to avoid a disaster on the ground, can be processed.

Professor Wickens couples these properties, required for situational awareness, into the representation of the pilot as an information processing system. Professor Wicken's system represents the pilot as a monitor of the airspace world, both inside and outside the cockpit. Therefore, a pilot is expected to readily process relevant events.

Plan continuation bias, or error, has been defined by the word perseveration. Perseveration is the pathology of persistent, repetition of a word, gesture, or act. In other words, decisions are not made by addressing the pros and cons of all choices available, but rather to occurrences that have been seen and experienced before. For example, and previously referred, Major Teagarden flew to Pittsburgh to attend the funeral of a fellow airman. The airman, Gary Swisher, was killed during an Air Force training mission in North Carolina a few days earlier. Present at the funeral was Swisher's pregnant widow. The question clearly surfaces, considering Major Teagarden's personal life of a wife and small children, did Swisher's death effect a survival bias to eject?

Aeronautical research has also shown that pilots, who are exposed to breakdowns, seek neither the cause of the problem, or

COGNITION, AERONAUTICAL DECISION MAKING AND SITUATIONAL AWARENESS

the very nature of the problem when failure-support assistance systems fail to provide validation. Major Teagarden, trying to re-light the engine 14-17 times or seek input from ATC (a form of CRM in a single pilot aircraft) or an alternate landing area, are examples that support this study. Major Teagarden consequently didn't seek and therefore couldn't unlock his train of thought (myopic) that the engine was not going to re-start. The word *orthogonal* helps define this bias as well. The length of the vector (or change of direction thereof) under the transformation can only equal the length of the original vector. In other words, if the transformation of the chain of events is going to occur, the link of transformative change has to be greater than the link being replaced.

> *The "Miracle on the Hudson" could not have succeeded, and the saving of 150 lives, had instrument meteorological conditions (IFR) not prevailed. It was only possible because Captain Sullenberger had visual meteorological conditions available at the time both engines quit operating.*

One of the best articles on the subject of situational awareness has been written and published for AOPA by Kenneth Stahl, MD, FACS 2/1/19. In summary, Stahl cites what happened to an AF pilot friend, Doug Downey when his F-117 experienced a flameout after takeoff. Doug told his friend that one of the engines flamed out, everything slowed down. Because of this he was able to process his situation calmly and relatively easily. Clinically speaking, it wasn't that things slowed down, it was that his brain sped up to process all the elements of his predicament. Only about 10% of people can react in this way to acute stress.

Doug accomplished this by planning and training for the PLAZ (possible loss of aircraft zone) scenario and the recovery from the wrong side of the power curve. Doug had mentally flown the exact same scenario hundreds of times. He ramped up his situational awareness before every flight. He would dare the aircraft to fail him. He knew the aircraft would fail. He was just waiting for it. He just needed to know how it would fail him and he would be ready.

Practical advice, to improve situational awareness (SA), is to picture it long before you need it in an emergency. Pre-live everything bad that might happen and then pre-live the solutions. Dare your aircraft to fail and use your imagination to plan for it.

It would be heretical not to mention factual, post impact to disregard of the pilot to have not engaged first responders with aircraft munition information. The impact site was less than a two-minute walk from the parking lot where the pilot safely parachuted. Had he communicated the negative armament status to the Fire Marshal, 4 lives would have been saved. The pilot cannot be cloaked by the immunity which is provided by the military. This was an inhumane, callous, and insensitive disregard for human lives and akin to a motor vehicle hit skip comparison. This can never be cleansed by military protocol. Period! "Sweet mercy is nobility's true badge." William Shakespeare.

Compare this intentional, deliberate, and encouraged absolution from ownership and fault by organizational culture, consequences are completely meaningless. Although avoiding comparing other world countries handling of similar catastrophes with more punitive measures, it must be mentioned that it is only intended for informational purposes and not an indictment.

A recent case, which happened on October 17, 2022 in Russia, does present a less hypocritical argument then the one presented herein. A Sukhoi-34 Strike Fighter Aircraft experienced an engine fire shortly after takeoff while on a training mission. The two pilots immediately ejected, allowing the pilotless aircraft to slam into a residential apartment building. The ensuring impact, and the predictable post-crash conflagration, left 13 fatalities and 19 civilians injured. Russian Investigative Committee began an investigation as a criminal matter that focused on violation of flight rules. The United Nations, which is the arbitrator of Russian's criminal code, indicated that pilots or ground crew could face charges for the "deprivation of liberty" because of actions or inactions related to the catastrophe. Article 44 of the Russian Federation Criminal Code clearly indicates that penalties apply to military and civilian personnel, alike. One has to ask themselves, when trying to comprehend the irony present between the democratically governed United States, and the totalitarian governed country of Russia as it relates to aviation accident investigations and the corresponding consequences thereof.

Also see NASA pilot cognition research center: https://human-factors.arc.nasa.gov/flightcognition/index.html

4
ADVANCEMENT OF AERONAUTICS AND SAFETY INFORMATION SHARING

IT MAKES SENSE, if military aircraft operations expose the civilian population to potential injury or harm, then the military should provide safety information in the public domain. Also, considering that the civilian population's taxes make the military possible, shouldn't there be more transparency expected of them? Opinions aside, the reality is that there is a plethora of private/nonmilitary sector scientists, researchers, professional investigative officials, engineers, and specialist who's experience and expertise is silenced because of executive privilege. This, unfortunately, was never more evident than when powered flight was in its infancy.

The Wright Brothers were granted a patent by the U.S. Patent Office in 1906. Their patent application, submitted in 1903, was premised on a detailed description, including drawings, of their flying machine. It must be noted that the Wright Brothers ultimate success was predicated on information, successes, and failures of just about all serious aircraft inventors that preceded them. However, let not this journey diminish the Wright Brothers genius of the three axis (pitch, roll, and yaw) control system they incorporated into their powered aircraft. It was during their autumn 1902 flight test campaign of their glider that their solution to three- axis control, linking roll and yaw, to mitigate the powerful adverse yaw effect that made their historic 1903 flight possible.

The brother's fascination with aeronautics began at an early age. Their father had bought the boys a toy helicopter, designed by Alphouse Penaud of France. Penaud had based the helicopter's design from one of Leonardo da Vinci's concepts. The brothers also followed the work of German engineer, Otto Lilienthal. Lilienthal preceded their efforts with glider aircraft design. In 1899 Wilbur wrote a letter to the Smithsonian Institution requesting any and all published information on the subject of flight. In his letter he explained that he wished to avail himself to all of the information already known by those who came before him. It appears, at least early on in the brothers' work, they were amenable to information sharing as documented in Wilbur's 1899 letter to the Smithsonian. To paraphrase Wilbur "Add my might to help on the future worker who will attain final success." Quite an intention. Interestingly, Wilbur did articulate this very sentiment in a letter to Octave Chanute. The letter read, in part, "I believe no financial profit will accrue to the inventor of the first flying machine, and that only those who are willing to give as to receive suggestions can hope to link their names with the honor of its discovery." However, the Wright Brothers would become more cautious of letting go of their ideas in years to come. But for now, they were willing to listen and conduct themselves as others in science and academia had been for generations. Evidence of this was Wilbur's reluctant participation in a scientific conference for the Society of Western Engineers. Reluctance because Wilbur's sister, Katharine, had to badger him to attend. She rightfully predicated that Wilbur would benefit from the networking opportunities that such a conference would present.

It has been documented that, had it not been for the brother's 1901 failures, remedies to future aeronautical dilemmas wouldn't have been achieved or achievement certainly delayed. One such remedy had to do with published material (tables) of Otto Lilienthal's concerning the coefficient of air pressure when describing its value in relation to lift created by the wing of an aircraft. While we're in the literary form of "splitting hairs", Wilbur found that Lilienthal's use of 0.005 as the coefficient of air pressure used in his formula defining lift was incorrect. Wilbur based his correction from cues developed by Professor Langley and the U.S. Weather Bureau, who both pegged K (air pressure) of the formula Lift = k S V2 C L, at 0.0032.

All in all, the Wright Brothers had mastered powered flight's most fundamental control mysteries in large part because of the successes and failures of their predecessors. However, it would be the decade long battle over patent infringements with Glenn Curtiss that would go down in the annals of aviation history as the most glaring example of how progress stops or slows because of privilege. The issues the Wright Brothers had with Glenn Curtiss involved the longitudinal control of an aircraft. That is, the ability of the aircraft to rotate (turn) on its longitudinal axis, with one wing descending while the other, simultaneously ascending. In this fashion, the aircraft rolls along an imaginary line, or axis, that runs from the tip of the nose through the tip of the tail. Curtiss-built aircraft used ailerons (small wing in French) on the outboard portion of the trailing edge of each wing. These ailerons, designed by Alexander Graham Bell, worked in opposite direction to each other. If the aircraft was put into a left turn, the left-wing aileron flipped upward while the aileron on the right wing simultaneously flipped downward. In essence, the upward movement of the left aileron causes the tip of the left wing to stall, causing more lift on the tip of the right wing and a corresponding raising of that wing. This ingenious design, which has stood the test of time for over a century, is still the primary aircraft roll control in effect today. The Wright Brothers viewed Curtiss' aileron control method the same as their patented wing warping method. In 1909, the brothers filed an infringement law suit against Glenn Curtiss.

As mentioned previously, the Wright Brothers were big fans of Otto Lilienthal. Otto had approached the science of flight mechanics in the same train of thought that the brothers envisioned, that is; to build a successful airplane, it was necessary to learn how to fly.[1] Otto Lilenthal totally understood this premise as evidenced by his commitment and courage during his test flights of his self-constructed gliders. Lilienthal's gliders were stable during straight and level flight, however maneuverability, and especially pitch control, would prove elusive and ultimately fatal. Otto, using the only method of control he could rely on and had relied on, hang gliding, couldn't overcome the counter force necessary to avoid the impact with the terrain that took his life.

The decades-long dispute, between Curtiss and the Wright Brothers drained Curtiss' aeronautical attention and locked the brothers into their own technology. Both by-products proved disastrous for all parties. World War I brought an end to the patent dispute. Ironically, it was the U.S. Government who urged aircraft manufacturers to put their difference aside and pool their collective know-hows for the sake of advancing the industry. The

ADVANCEMENT OF AERONAUTICS AND SAFETY INFORMATION SHARING

Manufacturers Aircraft Association, Inc. (MAA) entered the scene in the year of 1917. The organization's charter was simple: it published, for all to see, all the secret knowledge and data of aviation technology developed during the Great War. The premise was, it was believed, that it would provide the American public a fuller understanding of aviation and a deeper conviction of its growing place in our country. However, its main thrust, as envisioned by this post-war euphoria, was the application of aviation's advancement to the peaceful improvement to man's standard of living. In other words, how could the science of aviation fly food, mail, clothes, and our dearest relatives.

The MAA's effect on the fledgling aviation industry cannot be understated or underestimated in its efforts to move flight upwards. Part of its attractiveness, and future success, is how similar the undertakings toward safety and harmonization between military and civilian applications actually were. Both industries needed a central crossover medium of inclusion. The MAA's unquestionable success to the field of aeronautics, from its inception in 1917, until its culmination in 1975, came, in part, by the following:

- It put together a retention reservoir of manufacturers patents that allowed members unfettered access to technology licensing without fear of lawsuits.

- Standardized design of aircraft components and systems.

- Provided accessibility for new manufacturers to enter the market by capping aircraft production royalties.

- Present and future research and development in aviation was encouraged. This allowed the improved aspects to safety and performance of aircraft design.

Even after the sunset of the MAA in 1975, its successful legacy continued to prove useful. The MAA's model has more recently seen useful success in the semiconductor and digital industries.

So, a glaring question needs asking and answering. Could not, and should not the MAA's collaboration model be used for safety, investigative, and transparency proceedings and procedures, today? As the MAA was successful at making and sustaining progress after both World Wars for military and civilian aviation, it could certainly work towards eliminating the elephant in the room that presently exists. Eliminating the culture of secrecy, privilege, and indemnification for some (military) but full disclosure and openness for all others, has sustained a fair and repairable void.

Just as their contemporaries of several decades henceforth compared the Soviet Union's success with the space age launch and orbit of sputnik, the contemporaries of post-World War I realized that supremacy on land or sea was not of such great importance as supremacy of the air. However, putting forth a convincing theory would prove challenging. The early days produced committees that were further divided into sub-committees to deal with the development and organization of aircraft production. The aforementioned committees, early on, were unable to foresee any early development of aerial transports that could, by itself, keep the aircraft manufacturing industry alive. They (committees) did however, recognize that if the aircraft industry continued to service design and development of naval and military markets, then limited special considerations would be required for the civilian markets. Keeping this all into prospective, the race for mastery of the air had begun. In fact, Great Britain appropriated $100,000,000 to the effort over a 7-year period. In 1919, that was a significant sum.

A contemporary example of this void can be readily seen during the COVID Pandemic. Select organizations (FDA and Pfizer) were complicit, arguably, in the loss of millions of lives and the destruction of so many livelihoods. The FDA's self-regulatory privilege from releasing Freedom of Information Act (FOIA) to the public concerning pandemic information for an absurd period of 75 years, was borderline criminal. A fact that was adjudicated by the courts, but yet another example of hindsight being 20/20. These same self-regulated train wrecks on humanity also allowed vaccine pharmaceutical companies indemnification from liability.

The Federal Aviation Administration (FAA) has provided safety information sharing for decades. Airworthiness Directives (AD) are a safety channel to alert pilots and aircraft owners of deficiencies and manufacturing anomalies to alert and prevent subsequent occurrences in regards to unsafe equipment. The FAA also uses Service Difficulty Reports (SDR) which alerts aircraft operators of potential serious safety flaws.

An example of SDR's in action was prompted by TWA Flight 800. Flight 800 exploded soon after taking off from JFK Airport. Upon completion of the investigation, the likely cause was fuel vapor igniting inside the belly fuel tank by chaffed wiring.

A DC-10 engine separated from the mounting pylons at Chicago's O'Hare airport in 1979. The FAA found metal fatigue, that lead to pylon cracks, in other DC-10 aircraft at that time. Because of the complexities associated with Airworthiness Directives, they will be covered in greater detail later in the publication's section of suggested remediations.

This is not about building monuments to the dead. It's about sharing information for the purpose of safety for all of humanity. Safety information sharing is the only worthwhile requiem to the ten souls that perished on 10/20/1987. If transparency isn't the result, then these ten souls become forgotten victims and the forgotten victims' survivors become helpless for change to occur.

To reiterate, if military aircraft operations expose the civilian population to potential injury or harm, and not to mention their taxes that make the military possible, shouldn't there be more transparency afforded to them? Opinions aside, the reality is that there is a plethora of private/nonmilitary sector scientists, researchers, professional investigative officials, engineers, and specialists who's experience and expertise is silenced because of executive privilege.

Aeronautical information sharing has worked well in the civilian markets, but not so well in the military environment. This subject is covered more profoundly in the chapter Suggested Remediations. It takes a closer look at how these two markets, civilian and military, are really quite similar.

5
A-7 CORSAIR GENERAL, EMERGENCY AND EJECTION SEAT

THE VOUGHT A-7 CORSAIR II derives its name from the manufacturer's president.

Chance Milton Vought was an aviator and engineer who established his aircraft company on Long Island, New York in 1917. Together, with contributions from Birdseye B. Lewis, Vought Aircraft built the VE-7. A number of the VE-7's were delivered to the army before the end of World War I. The name Corsair was applied to a series of aircraft built for the navy by Vought Corporation between the World Wars. Most recognizable was the F-4U Corsair, made famous by Pappy Boyington of the Black Sheep Squadron of World War II's Pacific Theater.

The navy began a design competition in 1963 for a light-attack, carrier-based aircraft to replace the Douglas A-4 Skyhawk. The competition was meant to produce an aircraft that would carry a large ordinance payload and fly further than the A-4. In addition to Vought, Douglas, Grumman, and North American responded to the request for the proposal (RFP) to replace the A-4. In February 1964, the navy selected the Ling Temco Vought (LTV).

The A-7 production began on March 19, 1964 and continued through September of 1984. During the twenty plus years of production, 1,545 aircraft were made. The A-7D aircraft is a single-engine, single place, transonic light attack airplane manufactured by the Vought Aeronautics Division of LTV Aerospace Corporation. The aircraft has all weather combat capability and is equipped with the latest radar, navigational, communication, and weapon systems. The aircraft engine is a non-afterburner axial flow turbofan of Rolls-Royce design, manufactured by the Allison Division of General Motors. The wings are equipped with leading and trailing edge flaps. This combination of flaps allows the aircraft to fly at slower airspeeds, especially in the landing configuration. Aircraft stability is provided by an automatic flight control system. Flight control power is provided by two (three on some models) redundant hydraulic systems. Aircraft utilities, such as landing gear, speed brake, and flaps are operated off these systems.

The aircraft is 46.1 feet long with a 38.73 foot wing span and an empty weight of 22,000 pounds. Maximum takeoff weight of the aircraft is 46,000 pounds.

The A-7 was put into rapid production because Vought engineers based their design, in part, on the company's previous production aircraft, the F-8 Crusader. However, the high wing A-7 design (as opposed to the low wing F-8) was still closely related in geometry and physical size to the F-8.

The RAT, or ram air turbine, is purposely designed for emergency electrical and hydraulic power that, in normal operating conditions, is provided by the engine generator. This is a redundancy which allows the pilot of the aircraft to control various capabilities during in flight emergencies such as engine failure.

The A-7 is equipped with an emergency egress ejection system. The ESCAPAC IC-2 is made by Douglas Aircraft Company. Seat operation illustrations can be referenced with A-7 operating manual. (www.mach-one-manuals.net) The system uses a rocket catapult powered ejection seat consisting of several sub-systems. Sub-systems include the ejection seat, ejection seat sequencing system, canopy jettison controls, rocket catapult, parachute, survival kit container, and restraint seat adjustment.

The survival kit contains a life raft that can be automatically or manually deployed by the pilot if egress was made over water. The system provides the pilot the ability to safely escape the aircraft in the event of a catastrophic aircraft incident and can be activated from zero altitude and from zero airspeed up to tens of thousands of feet and up to 650 knots of airspeed. The ground level capability of the ejection system can be utilized in the event of aircraft overrun into a hazardous area or in other situations in which sufficient flying speed is not available.

It should be noted that the Douglas Aircraft Company's chief competitor is a British company, Martin-Baker. Martin-Baker sends a congratulatory letter to any pilot who successfully ejects using one of the seats (Sullenberger). Ejection capability makes pilots think (or not) in different trains of thought per Sullenberger. The International Journal of Trendy Research in Engineering and Technology, (IJTRET) published an article titled, Principle and Applications of Ejection Seat in Aeronautics, by J. Manjunath and D. JayaybalaKrishnan; October 2019. The authors used Issac Newton's Second Law of Physics to describe the necessary factors required for safe ejection seat operations. Newton's second law applies in the context that suggests what force would be necessary to produce the acceleration of a given mass (seat and pilot) to rapidly extract the pilot. The catapult, or the initial system activity, removes the seat from the aircraft via an explosive charge.

However, if the explosive catapult is the exclusive means for seat ejection, it would impose an unsustainable G-force of 15-20 on the pilot's body. Therefore, the catapult explosive charge takes a very short amount of time just to separate the seat from the aircraft. Quickly after the seat catapult explosion, rocket sustainers provide final pilot and aircraft separation and a more anatomically safter G factor of 5-10 on the human occupant.

Only in-flight emergency procedures will be discussed, since the occurrence of October 20, 1987 and the actions taken therein, were primarily restricted to this configuration. These emergency procedures are summarized from information contained in the A-7 Flight Operations Manual. The manual exists in the public domain and references to the manual information is factual and unbiased.

The U.S. Military classifies in-flight loss of engine operation as a flameout. This is a suitable description since turbojet engines operate via the combination of compressed air, fuel, and the ignition that produces the thrust required for flight. Section 3 of the A-7 Flight Operations Manual provides all of the emergency information needed by the pilot. This includes how the pilot is expected to respond to emergencies.

For the sake of brevity, the following information pertains to flameout approaches and landings. Again, the purpose of narrowing the emergency focus is to stay on task with the matter at hand. The manual makes clear, in no uncertain terms, that a pilot *"SHALL NOT" attempt a flameout approach to landing* under the following conditions:

- When the approach to the landing area is over a heavily populated area.

- Weather conditions must not impede the pilot in establishing a proper approach to landing pattern.

- The pilot must be able to visually, at minimum, ascertain a pattern altitude of 3000 feet above ground level.

What is paradoxical, is that the aforementioned information will always be provided to the pilot by Air Traffic Control (ATC), prior to commencing an approach. However, the military, in the same section of the manual, adds a contradictory note. The note instructs the pilot to eject if during the approach conditions do not appear ideal for a successful landing. There are many contradictions contained in the emergency section of the Flight Operations Manual. I contend therefore, it is imperative that these contradictions be exposed with conviction. Accordingly, and most appropriately, they have been delineated in the book's chapter of suggested remediations.

As mentioned previously, in limited circumstances, in-flight restarts might be attempted. However, after several attempts to restart becomes glaringly apparent that success is futile, the pilot should, without delay, be immediately compelled to seek alternative measures to mitigate future flame-out carnage.

The moral, ethical, and professional reasoning for a pilot to eject in a civilian populated area has been constantly thematic throughout this book. However, it will be sufficed to say that a pilot's decision to eject while over a populated area carries with it extremely terrible odds. Innocent civilians will be seriously injured or killed. Scrupulous adherence to training, operating procedures, military and civilian aviation rules and regulations cannot become randomly interpretated. Although the litany on the use of the ejection seat is one of simple common sense, one should not overlook the primary purpose of the seat's application. It was designed and implemented for only military combat aircraft. Military jet fighter pilots must expect to be fired upon by enemy air and ground forces. The result of these combat activities, whether over land or water, could easily damage the aircraft, and make it necessary for the pilot to activate the ejection seat. No other military, civilian airlines, corporate and general aviation aircraft are similarly equipped. The flight crews of those aforementioned aircraft must stay with the aircraft. Staying with a crippled aircraft, and ultimately providing control and potentially avoiding inhabited areas, can and does save lives.

6
SUGGESTED REMEDIATIONS

AS THIS CHAPTER BEGINS, it is important to know that Air Force Flight Officer Training Program lack adequate ditching, swimming, and water survival training. Navy and Marine pilots have more confidence in surviving a ditched aircraft. Navy and Marine pilots must swim one mile in full flight gear. There is much more emphasis on open water operation because of the obvious reason that the majority of operations are conducted in or near its proximity. Ditching an aircraft in water neutralizes a pilot-less aircraft. United States Naval Aviators, who have experienced ditching, or performing a water egress, associate their positive outcome on the first-class water survival training they had received.

There should be a drastic simplification of the Naval Air Training and Operating Procedures Standardization (NATOPS) pilot operating manual. Seven hundred pages is way too long. High altitude enroute charts have poor or very little depiction of actual geography/topography, which confuses pilot reality and situational awareness.

There needs to be more emphasis on stress and circadian rhythms. The A.F. commanding officers that allowed a pilot to fly to a funeral of a pilot's best friend, made a terrible decision. Life changing events can, and do have negative effects on human performance. Matters such as divorce, money difficulties, problems at home, death of a relative or friend, and career changes are but a few examples of life's negative events. Organizations need to reach out and engage with third party entities that have conducted these efforts of empirical research on human vs. machine integration and adopt their best practices. NASA, as an example, has a division that is exclusively tasked with the human to machine integration for improvement of safety matter considerations for the aerospace community.

The author's remediations are based on the inevitability that more accidents will occur and sharing information is critical. Fair, unbiased investigating, performed cooperatively, with an independent body, should have the ability to share (seek remedies) information without barriers. The AF/military needs to adopt a more open and transparent investigative process that is more closely aligned with the NTSB (civilian) process model, keeping everyone, especially families, honestly informed. Possible problems can only be solved when they are known to exist.

The Pilot Operating Manual, aircraft specific, contains important emergency procedures. These procedures must be followed scrupulously. Notable examples are the prohibition of dead-stick landings in populated areas, or attempting dead-stick landings in instrument meteorological conditions. There should be limits on the number of engine restart attempts, planning for safe areas to allow for emergency landings or "ditching." Fuel must be dumped to mitigate post-crash fire. Pilot must be able to use ATC as a partner to create a crew resource management (CRM) and functionality enhancement. (two heads are better than one). Many contradictions, to emergency procedures, are present in the

SUGGESTED REMEDIATIONS

Flight Operation Manual. These contradictions, sadly, escape, and or avoid, the paramount safety of civilians and the prevention of casualties caused, in part, by their own ambiguity. All of the above, when not executed pursuant to published procedures, are examples that can lead to "perseveration" and myopic tendencies. Simply put, increased attention to remediate any flawed and complex construct fosters safer and greater performance.

The following are examples of contradictions gleaned from the manual:

- The confirmation that some unsuccessful flameout landings occurred because of the distracting influence caused by the pilot's attempt to air-start the engine. Military leaders have made it abundantly clear that pilots should prepare and precondition their cognitive abilities and mindset to begin preparations for alternative actions after five to seven attempts to re-start a dead engine. These alternative actions, as directed, must include off-airport locations. There are, for the most part, numerous locations that can be utilized. Rural farmland could readily provide a suitable unpopulated location. Bodies of water, whether it be a river, lake, or a larger area such as an ocean, all have a greater ability to neutralize a post-crash inferno.

- Fuel must be jettisoned, from aircraft fuel tanks, prior to attempting a dead-stick landing. This is only common sense and represents a basic act that benefits the pilot as well as those unsuspecting people on the ground. This would obviously remove the enormous potential for a post impact fire, explosion and in turn improve the survivability for anyone in harm's way.

- Attempting a dead-stick landing in instrument meteorological conditions should be prohibited! In order to perform a successful landing, either with power or without power, a pilot must be able to have *visual* cues of the landing area available. These *visual* cues must be a factor that heavily influences the success or failure of the attempted "landing." When visual cues are available, it allows the pilot to adjust the aircraft's *position*, *altitude*, and *proximity* to other aircraft that might be present within the airport vicinity of the recommended landing site. It also provides visual information to the surrounding area in the event that abandonment of the approach becomes necessary.

There cannot be a single factor that would lead to a positive outcome for an emergency landing when visual cues are not available. Of all prohibitions to be scrupulously observed by pilots faced with an in-flight emergency situation, the presence of instrument meteorological conditions has inexorably preordained the outcome to one of failure! This is exactly the reason it is prefaced in the operating manual as, "*shall not be attempted.*"

There needs to be congressional revisitation of Title 5 USC and the corresponding immunity it provides. As previously referenced, Title 5 USC provides for U.S. Government Agencies a privileged status from release to the public of information an

SUGGESTED REMEDIATIONS

agency deems to be proprietary. This remediation will be very difficult to realize. For obvious reasons, significant change will require congressional intervention. Relatively sporadic incidences and lower numbers in causalities, all unfortunately quickly forgotten by the public as a whole due in part to "short memory" syndrome. It might be a different set of circumstances if, for example, an aircraft crashed into a stadium filled with tens of thousands or more spectators. Circumstances might also significantly change if an important politician or family member were killed or badly injured.

Instead of investigators assigning blame for what caused an accident, they might instead exercise objectivity to determine what could have prevented it.

As referenced above, concerning the NTSB investigative procedures and protocols it adheres to, civil aviation's religious doctrine of safety cannot be broken. In this context, the Federal Aviation Administration (FAA) works arduously in tandem with all entities responsible for all aviation activities and their safety. One epic piece of that safety contingent is its formalized process of notification and a regulatory supported program known as the Airworthiness Directive Notification Process (AD).

ADs are issued and circulated to <u>civil aircraft</u> manufacturers, airlines, operators, and owners when an aircraft's component(s) has been identified as a potential hazard to the operational safety that can lead to catastrophic consequences. These are not benign or rudimentary notifications, but well documented notices brought on when a similar adverse condition has been verified or that could possibly exist, within a fleet of the same make and model of aircraft.

Unfortunately, it may take an accident with the loss of lives to uncover the underlying deficiencies before antidotal corrective action can be carried out.

Recent horrific examples of after the fact corrective activities do not require in-depth research to gain an understanding of this reality.

There were two such accidents close in proximity to one another. They both involved, at the time, the newest version of the venerable Boeing 737. Boeing named it the B-737-8 MAX.

An Indonesian Airline B-737-8 MAX aircraft crashed on 10/29/2018. The catastrophic accident resulted in 189 fatalities. There were no survivors. The second accident, less than 6 months after the Indonesian mishap, involved an Ethiopian Airline B-737-8 MAX. All 157 persons onboard perished and post-crash investigation determined the cause to be identical as the 10/29/2018 accident.

Then came the reports from other pilot operators of the B-737-8 MAX aircraft that flight crewmembers had experienced flight control oscillation incidents that disrupted aerodynamic stability and temporary loss of control. By this time, the manufacturer and the regulators could not speculate any longer to the fact that this situation was beyond isolated.

The FAA moved in swiftly by issuing an Emergency AD on 3/13/2019, three days after the Ethiopian Airliner accident, that ultimately grounded all B-737-8 MAX aircraft.

The post investigative results determined that a sensor that supplies aircraft angle of attack (AOA) information to the maneuvering characteristic augmentation system (MCAS) malfunctioned. This system failure resulted in an uncontrolled downward

SUGGESTED REMEDIATIONS

pitch attitude of the aircraft even after pilot induced counter controlling inputs to the contrary.

The reason I have presented this information, is because the U.S. Military and the U.S. Government operate similar civilian production aircraft that are comprised of the very same components as their civilian counterparts. An example of this civil to military aircraft crossover is the U.S. Navy's P-8A Poseidon. The P-8A is manufactured by Boeing. Boeing's commercial airline model designation, however, is B-737-8FV because it's part of the civilian production aircraft widely used by the airlines. In fact, Boeing's marketing efforts are used to entice the Navy's purchasing interests, so the aircraft shares an 86% commonality with the civilian B-737. However, if the military experiences safety related anomalies with these aircraft, they are not required, and therefore do not provide this information to the civilian operators via the AD protocol. Information that could possibly prevent serious accidents is of no concern, and literally ignored by the Navy! This is a ruinous military policy! The B-737 and P-8A comparison is but one example of military and civilian crossover application similarities. These crossover equipment applications are far too numerous and distracting to bring forward. However, the implications cannot be ignored and are no less satisfying of their lethality.

As with so many changes that are more pedestrian and commonly recognizable, technological advances in aviation have immensely improved safety. As numerous as these advancements are, the presentation of but a few should serve to bring a somewhat antidotal prophylaxis to a sometimes error prone endeavor. One technological advancement has been with aircraft instrumentation.

Analog instruments, such as the altimeter, the turn and slip indicator, heading indicator, and airspeed indicator, have been in use for several decades. Their longevity has been largely attributable to the relatively simplistic design and unwavering effectiveness. However, in addition to technologically advanced instrumentation, some aircraft are still equipped with the old, tried and true, instrumentation as backup in case of technically advanced instrumentation failure. Aviation, even in the twenty first century, has been about redundancies.

It must be noted that much information throughout this publication, takes on a rather pedantic complexion. This, however, has not been by design or compulsion. Every detail of every researchable pathway traveled inextricably led to the same means to its same end.

Aviation, both civil and military, must tear down any cloak of "privileged secrecy" and work together, mutually, for the safety and advancement of one of mankind's greatest achievements. It is with the sincerest of human characteristics, the characteristic of selflessness that will get us there. Anything less would be meaningless.

The indelible irony to achieving this elusive safety objective is not dependent on funding or something more operationally distractive and destructive like a preordained recruitment policy based on racial or gender identities. The idea that just because eighty two percent of military pilots happened to be of the male gender, and therefore the fabricated excuse that change is required, smacks as pure "wokeness."

The military needs an exorcism of its behavior and of its culture. It's very difficult, if not impossible, to effectuate positive change when military senior leadership knows that no matter the carnage and destroyed families a mishap has caused, the post-accident investigation will never see the light that the court of public opinion rightfully provides.

A more recent case and point, validating the need for positive investigatory change, happened in September, 2023. A Marine Corps F-35 joint strike fighter aircraft crashed in rural South Carolina after the pilot ejected. The circumstances that lead to the pilot's ejection were quite remarkable. And, as was later determined from military investigations, caused by pilot error. Afterall, how could an operating, pilot-less, aircraft travel some 60 miles and then crash in a rural area and somehow not be someone's fault?

The same question was asked of the Marine Corps by South Carolina Representative Nancy Mace. "How in the hell do you lose an F-35? When there is ongoing situation which potentially threatens public safety, the Pentagon has an obligation to keep citizens and their representatives informed."

Of course, the publicly released safety report from the military was highly redacted. But, again, it highly underscores the pressing need for permanent legislative change to have any significant change for public safety.

As previously referenced, but extremely worth revisiting, the proffered remediations are not exhaustive and some could have actually been effectuated. However, if only one remedy could be chosen and implemented, by catching the right decision maker's eye, the legislative component would certainly be of invaluable worth. The will, to open the door to the future of public safety, starts publicly!

Lastly, no one, not military nor civilian persons should ever leave the scene of an accident! Anyone who has had some or all of the responsibility for causation of an accident or mishap, bears the moral obligation of remaining at the scene. In many instances, the person responsible may have lifesaving information no one else has.

7
10 SOULS

IT IS WITH the complete realization that mere words could never assuage the grief experienced and endured, over the event of October 20, 1987, by surviving family members or of the community. Conversations took place with some surviving family members, but not all, to learn more about each victim. Consolation, if possible, would be knowing that each victim's life provided an everlasting and unwavering commitment to arrive at the truth. It is with the utmost sincerity, by this author, that each reader will share the same objective.

EMMA JEAN BROWNLEE, 37
Housekeeper, Ramada Inn
Emma J. Brownlee was born in Mississippi on September 3, 1950.

Most of Emma's family lived in Mississippi, but Emma lived with her son, Michael (nineteen years old at the time of the tragedy) in Indianapolis.

Emma was a loving mother, friend and diligent worker. She was buried in Aberdeen, Mississippi.

RUTH KATHERINE COX, 33
Dining Room Manager, Ramada Inn

Ruth Katherine Cox was born in Jasper, Indiana on September 24, 1954 to William and Ruth Cox. Ruth had three siblings. She graduated High School in Jasper. Her father, William was an attorney in Jasper as well.

Ruth was the Dining Room Manager for the Indianapolis Ramada Inn. Her family was traveling in Georgia at the time of her death.

Ruth K. Cox was honored and laid to rest at Haysville Community Cemetery in Haysville, Indiana.

CHRISTOPHER LEE EVANS, 21
Desk Clerk, Bellman

Christopher Lee Evans was born in Indianapolis, Indiana on November 29, 1965 to Lindo and Barbara Evans. Christopher had one brother, Mark.

Christopher graduated from Decatur Central High School in 1984 and had studied at IUPUI (Indiana University-Purdue University Indianapolis). He was one class short of an associate's degree in computer programming at Lockyear College.

Christopher worked at the Ramada Inn in Indianapolis as a bellman and front desk clerk. He worked there for a little more than one year.

Christopher was working the front desk when the crash occurred. He called his mother when the crash happened and said "I think I'm going to be ok" …..then the phone went dead.

Christopher Evans was a kind and caring person and a friend to many.

BETH LOUISE GOLDBERG, 30
Assistant Sales Director, Ramada Inn

Beth Louise Goldberg was born in Indianapolis, Indiana on August 5, 1957 to Robert and Harriet Goldberg. She had two sisters.

Beth attended and graduated from North Central High School in 1975. She then graduated from Arizona State University with a degree in Textiles and Clothing in 1979.

After graduating college, Beth moved and lived out of state for awhile before moving back to Indianapolis. She worked as the Assistant Sales Director for the Ramada Inn in Indianapolis for three months before her death.

Beth Goldberg was a good daughter, wonderful sister and great friend to many.

BRENDA JOYCE HENRY, 26
Housekeeper, Ramada Inn

Brenda Joyce Henry was born in Martinsville, Indiana on February 3, 1961 to William and Charlotte Henry. After moving from Martinsville to Indianapolis, Brenda attended Crispus Attucks and Washington High Schools. Brenda had four siblings. She lived with her parents and nine-month-old son, Travis. Brenda was engaged to be married.

Brenda thought about staying home on October 20, 1987, because her son, Travis was teething and sick, but she decided not to because she didn't like to miss work. She needed the money for her son.

According to family and friends, Brenda Henry was a very popular, friendly and outgoing woman.

NARINDER S. KANWAR, 41
Assistant Manager/Financial Officer, Controller, Ramada Inn

Narinder S. Kanwar was born in India on February 3, 1946. He had four sisters and three brothers.

Narinder worked as an engineer in Nigeria before moving to the United States. He worked in Florida and Ohio before making his home in Indianapolis with his wife, Saroj and their three children. He was the Assistant Manager and Controller at the Ramada Inn in Indianapolis.

Narinder was known for his kind heart, contagious smile and artistic nature.

DAWN ESCHELLE "SHELLY" MARTIN, 19
Front Desk Clerk, Ramada Inn

Dawn Eschelle Martin was born in Columbus, Indiana on July 11, 1968 to Larry and Sheryl Martin. She attended Columbus North High School and graduated in 1986.

Everyone called Dawn by her middle name, "Shelly" (Eschelle). She was planning to marry Michael Taylor in the fall. She earned a scholarship to study art at Indiana University-Purdue University Indianapolis (IUPUI). Her dream was to be a graphic designer.

Dawn "Shelly" Martin was fun loving, cheerful and a joy to be around.

ALLEN DALE MANTOR, 18
Houseman, Ramada Inn

Allen Dale Mantor was born in Lebanon, Indiana on February 26, 1969 to Gerald and Mavis Mantor. Allen had nine siblings.

Allen attended Cascade High School and was employed as a houseman at the Ramada Inn in Indianapolis.

Allen enjoyed making models and spent much of his time playing baseball. He was close to his family, especially his older brother, Gerald, who, ironically, served in the United States Air Force.

Allen Mantor had a kind, giving heart and a focused work ethic. He always wanted to do things the "right way".

MARY STUART MARSH, 29
Director of Sales, Ramada Inn

Mary Stuart Marsh was born in Columbus, Indiana on September 26, 1958 to Glen and Kathleen Stuart. She graduated from Decatur Central High School in 1976.

Mary was the Director of Sales for the Indianapolis Ramada Inn. According to her co-workers, friends and family, Mary was a kind and thoughtful woman. She was a diligent worker, friend to many, a loving wife, and a caring mother to her two children, Stuart and Heather (from a previous marriage). She lived in Mars Hill, Indiana with her husband, Kevin Marsh.

Prior to her death on October 20, 1987, Mary was offered a job where she would have made more money than her Director of Sales position with the Ramada Inn, but she turned that offer down. She was a mother first, and a career woman second.

THOMAS CHARLES MURRAY, 37
Regional Sales Manager for Haynes International in Kokomo, Indiana

Thomas Charles Murray was born in Cleveland, Ohio on August 21, 1950 to Robert and Josephine Murray. He grew up in Maple Hts., Ohio and graduated from St. Peter Chanel High School in 1968. He graduated college in 1972, later married Florence and had a family. They lived in Carmel Indiana. Tom was the Regional Sales Manager for Haynes International in Kokomo, Indiana.

On the morning of October 20, 1987, Tom stopped at the Ramada Inn in Indianapolis to make a phone call. After his call, as he was leaving and reaching the parking lot, he saw the plane barreling down towards him. He avoided contact, but was engulfed in flames from the fireball that imploded the lobby of the building. He suffered burns over 95 percent of his body. He held on for nine days, then died on October 29, 1987.

Tom Murray was a great friend, son, husband and father.

EPILOGUE

BRUCE TEAGARDEN came back East, from his base at Nellis AFB, NV, to attend the funeral of his friend, Gary Swisher, and to use the trip as an opportunity to see family in Mt. Morris, PA. The AF allowed the use of the A-7 (Corsair) to Pittsburgh, for the purpose of flight training. Gary Swisher was flying in a training exercise, in a rural area of North Caolina a few days earlier, when the F-4 aircraft he was flying in as the operation/weapons officer flew directly into the ground at night, because the pilot in command lost situational awareness. The accident was the result of the pilot becoming confused by night operations and the corresponding loss of a reliable horizon along with the failure to use aircraft instrumentation to verify altitude and position relative to the ground's proximity.

The funeral was a somber affair. The closed casket was reflective of a military serviceman killed in the line of duty. A grieving, pregnant, widow, left to pick up what pieces remained. Whether these events contributed to Bruce Teagarden's mindset a few days later can be debated. What is known of human conditions at the time of immense pressure/stress can be proven. Circadian rhythms and personal emotional stress have had negative effects on pilot performance, and that is well documented by the AF, themselves. The effects of life-stress on pilot performance are the title of a research article written by James A. Young at the Ames Research Center:

Life-stress is defined as physical and psychological symptoms. These symptoms include muscle tension, worry or preoccupation, disrupted sleep/fatigue, change in appetite, alteration in social interactions such as withdrawal, irritability, or difficulty concentrating. These are often a product of difficult life circumstances. Among those circumstances are relationship difficulties, financial worries, health concerns, bereavement issues, work related problems, and separation from family.

Major Teagarden's mind set on the morning of October 20, and all the events that led him to Pittsburgh and Indianapolis airports, "re-conditioned" his response to the engine malfunction.

He set himself up for an engine-out landing when his mind was pre-conditioned to egress. Had he planned for either, not both options, the outcome would have been much different. Here are the reasons the outcomes would have been different, especially in Instrument Meteorological Conditions (IMC), prevalent at the time:

- The engine-out landing procedures would have required the pilot to attempt to restart the engine. That task required a sequence of ten (10) steps each needing 25-45 seconds to perform.

- Furthermore, in order for the pilot to have had a chance of restarting the engine, the engine had to be "windmilling" to 15% RPM, which needed a minimum of 300

EPILOGUE

Knots Indicated Airspeed (KIAS) to produce that 15%. All of the above caused a rapid loss of altitude.

- The pilot should had been planning for a dead stick landing in an unpopulated area. He also should had been dumping fuel knowing very well that his engine was not going to reignite. This would also minimize an explosion if he had to eject.

- The A-7 was capable, with auxiliary power, provided by the RAT/EPP, of dumping 300 gallons per minute through the 28 volt/dc bus. RAT/EPP provides both ac/dc power and hydraulics.

- It will be noted here that each A-7 wing fuel tanks holds half of the total aircraft fuel capacity of 10,173 pounds or 1500 gallons of JP-4 jet fuel. Therefore, each wing held 750 gallons.

- The aircraft was capable of dumping 750 gallons in less than two and a half minutes.

- If a dead-stick landing procedure alone had been Bruce Teagarden's mind set, then it is conceivable the casualties, especially Tom Murray's 90% burn coverage, could had been avoided.

- The major would have also had two to three minutes to request ATC vectors to an unpopulated area.

These are the facts. The reader should draw their own conclusions.

- The pilot's actions that lead to the disaster.

- An Instrument Meteorological Condition (IMC) dead-stick was attempted.

- The engine re-start was attempted 14-17 times.

- He didn't engage (in fact disengaged) the scene and first responders. The Fire Marshal noted two or three victims had high concentrations of carbon monoxide, suggesting they suffered terribly for a number of minutes before expiring.

- He let "politics" control the event after the disaster.

- He didn't jettison fuel before approaching Indianapolis without power.

- He refused to consider ditching or vectors to a rural area. He also declined an alternate airport at Terra Haute.

- His operation manual prohibits dead-stick landing attempts in populated areas or in IMC conditions.

- His manual prohibited engine re-light attempts if they were unsuccessful after 5-7 attempts.

EPILOGUE

- As previously mentioned, the military investigative processes included two separate investigations, one public and one privileged.

Many more recent events of pilots ejecting have also occurred. There was one in Russia that caused numerous causalities of people on the ground. The other was near Charleston, South Carolina and miraculously did not cause any fatalities. Other military pilots have faced similar fates as Bruce Teagarden. On May 9, 1981 at Hill Air Force Base, Ogden, Utah the Airforce precision flying Thunderbirds were performing. It was the 40th anniversary of the Air Force base public airshow. The spectators, it was estimated, numbered 80,000. During a low altitude, tandem routine, Captain David Hauck's T-38 Talon aircraft experienced what was described as engine failure. Witnesses said that after passing over the spectator area, the aircraft attempted a turn towards the runway. With landing gear extended, the aircraft hit the ground and cartwheeled before coming to rest on a small hill in a field away from the spectator's area. Local stories from the Standard-Examiner and fellow pilots said that Captain Hauck could have ejected. However, he remained with the aircraft to control it so it wouldn't harm or kill spectators and gave up his life honorably in the process.

An Air Force Thunderbird pilot, Captain Charlie Carter, 33 of San Antonio, Texas, piloted his disabled T-38 Talon aircraft safely past hundreds of camper vehicles rather than eject. Captain Carter guided the aircraft to avoid hitting an area of campers present for the rodeo and airshow. Captain Carter instructed his crewmember, Sargeant Ted Foster, 27 of Charlotte, North Carolina, to eject moments before crashing. Sargeant Foster survived, thanks to the selflessness of Captain Carter. Carter guided and controlled his aircraft through a 30-foot gap of camper vehicles before crashing into a paddock area of livestock. He too perished, honorably. (Traverse City Record-Eagle, July 26, 1977)

During a research period for the manuscript, one particular interview with a former military pilot proved startling. When referencing the events of 10/20/1987, the former military pilot cautioned on making a determination of blaming Bruce Teagarden's decision to eject. The word used, to convey this line of thought, was to be "dispassionate". The examples, referenced above, of pilots staying with their aircraft to avoid casualties on the ground, are quite different than the event of 10/20/1987. Captains Hauck and Carter only had mere seconds in the decision process. Bruce Teagarden had over <u>eight minutes</u> and several options of availability in which to choose. He also had resources such as ATC, copious amounts of unpopulated rural farm land, and of course, large suitable bodies of water to ditch the aircraft. Unfortunately for the ten victims, Bruce Teagarden did not avail himself and his aircraft to these potentially more suitable alternatives. In a sense, it is somewhat understandable of the decision he made to attempt a dead-stick landing at Indianapolis International Airport. The radio transcripts, between Teagarden and ATC, reflect the sort of abdication of pilot-in-command (PIC) responsibilities that Teagarden, and only Teagarden, could execute. Again, keeping in mind, ATC's regulated mandate is separation of aircraft within the airspace and that of advisory assistance for the pilots. ATC cannot fly the aircraft for the pilot. ATC does, however, have the capability to accurately identify all topographical features present

EPILOGUE

on the ground below the aircraft. It only takes a request, by the PIC, and ATC can provide the information, including vectors to the requested area(s). After 5-7 attempts to re-start the engine unsuccessfully and the fact that the operation, in direct prohibition of Air Force policies, was attempted in instrument meteorological conditions. Teagarden would have had sufficient time to force land/ditch in an unpopulated area.

As referenced earlier, to subdue the human emotion and remain dispassionate to what took place on 10/20/1987 and exonerating the person directly responsible, would be akin to the acquittal of a confessed murderer. But those who are curious readers and much, much more importantly, surviving relatives of the deceased, it is of the utmost importance to digest the foregoing and hopefully reach some semblance of well-deserved closure. The information that has been provided is factual. The alternatives suggested that would have prevented the event of 10/20/1987 belong strictly and exclusively to the aeronautically educated and experienced author. It is of imperative importance that after personal contemplation and reflection of the actions, or lack thereof, by Bruce Teagarden in accordance with the sworn oath he took and affirmed as a United States Air Force Officer, that I have tried to provide such closure to the victims of the event.

It must be brought to bear, in the author's opinion, that Major Teagarden was provided with a modicum of self-redemption had he so chosen. If the reader recalls, early on, four victims were hiding in an adjacent laundry room. As the Fire Chief had indicated, these victims survived for several post impact minutes. This had been determined by way of forensic autopsies which confirmed high levels of carbon monoxide in the victim's lungs.

These levels were consistent with living human functionality of 4-7 minutes. Again, if you recall earlier, the Fire Chief prevented his crew from search and rescue operations because it had not been known whether the aircraft was carrying any ordinances or armament. The redemption Major Teagarden was offered quickly evaporated when, under the presumption of the call he made to a superior officer, he was instructed to stand down and disengage from the accident site. Of course, by doing so, he sealed the fate of the four victims trapped in the laundry room. The humane and surely instinctive reaction, orders notwithstanding, was to jog less than a minute to the accident site and inform the Fire Chief that the aircraft was not armed. Afterall, he had previously violated Air Force procedures when trying to land at Indianapolis Airport in the first place. Just following orders, in this instance, does not provide the vail of indemnification that would allow him to hide forever. Even a semblance of ownership, mea culpa if you will, would have somewhat lessened the pain for the victim's survivors. Attitudes, as expressed by one AF investigative officer of the 10/20/1987 crash: "We looked into the facts surrounding the incident. The A-7 is a single-engine aircraft. The gearbox failed, and the single engine stopped its ability to produce thrust, and that was pretty much it" ......it's NOT pretty much it!

GODSPEED TO THE TEN SOULS OF OCTOBER 20, 1987!

ADDITIONAL RESOURCES

THE READER CAN USE the links provided to access and reference additional information that has been cited in the book.

A-7 Corsair Aircraft Flight Manual provides complete normal and emergency operating specifications and illustrations: https://archive.org/details/T.O.1A7D1FlightManualA7D20091972/pagen273/mode/2up

Indianapolis Star Newspaper contains original articles from the days immediately after the accident: https://indystar.newspapers.com/

FAA Aeronautical Chart Products. Descriptive illustrations show the Sectional and Enroute Charts and their un-commonality: https://www.faa.gov/air_traffic/flight_info/aeronav/productcatalog/

United States Fire Administration, (Ramada Inn Air Crash and Fire Wayne Township, IN) Technical Report: http://www.usfa.dhs.gov/

Title 5, United States Code, Government Organization and Employees, Part 1, Chapter 5, Subchapter II, Section 552. Public and nonpublic information (FOIA): www.uscode.house.gov/browse

NASA Ames Research Center, Human Systems Integration, Aviation Safety Reporting System (ASRS). Voluntary reporting of safety incidents, events or situation. Information is used for identifying deficiencies and discrepancies for remedial purposes: https://humansystems.arc.nasa.gov

ENDNOTES

Preface
1 Michael J. Lynch, Colonel USAF Mishap Report
2 Randolph E. Kirby, United States Fire Administration

Chapter
1   Alan E. Diehl

Chapter 2
1   OPNAV 3750.6R

Chapter 3
1 Wiley Post: Wikipedia
2 Robert Alkov, PH. D

Chapter 4
1   F.E.C. Culick, Cal Tech

ABOUT THE AUTHOR

MARK F. MURRAY is the son of a World War II veteran. Mark's father was an avionics technician (B-25s) for the United States Army Air Corp, 12th Airforce, of the Mediterranean Theater in North Africa and Corsica. After the war, Mark's father worked for and retired from Eastern Airlines.

Not surprising, then, that Mark followed his father's passion for aviation. Mark is a former federal investigator for the US Department of Justice, a commercial pilot, former certified flight instructor, and FAA safety counselor. Through a career of government service and self-immersion into the field of aeronautics, Mark realized the need for positive change, especially when it came to safety. The approach to safety, as it was and still remains, has been of paramount importance. He is a graduate of Malone University with a bachelor's degree in business administration.

www.ingramcontent.com/pod-product-compliance
Lightning Source LLC
LaVergne TN
LVHW041548070426
835507LV00011B/992